Quotations to Cheer You Up

When the World is Getting You Down

Quotations
to Cheer You Up
When the World is
Getting You Down

COMPILED BY
Allen Klein

ILLUSTRATED BY
Monica Sheehan

WINGS BOOKS • NEW YORK

Edited by Jeanette Green

Copyright © 1991 by Allen Klein

Grateful acknowledgment is made to United Technologies Corporation for permission to reprint the quotation on page 160. © 1982 by United Technologies Corporation.

This 1994 edition is published by Wings Books,
an imprint of Random House Value Publishing, Inc.
280 Park Avenue, New York, New York 10017,
by arrangement with Sterling Publishing Company, Inc.

Wings Books and colophon are trademarks of Random House Value Publishing, Inc.

Random House
New York • Toronto • London • Sydney • Auckland
http://www.randomhouse.com/

Printed and bound in the United States of America

Library of Congress Cataloging-in-Publication Data
Quotations to cheer you up when the world is getting you down / [compiled by] Allen Klein.
p.   cm.
Previously published: New York : Sterling Pub. Co., 1991.
Includes index.
ISBN 0-517-10014-2
1. Quotations. 2. Wit and humor. I. Klein, Allen.
PN6084.H8Q67   1994
082—dc20   93-29512
CIP

16 15 14 13 12 11 10

*For cousin Bernice
who is never at a loss for words
(and most of them uplifting)*

CONTENTS

INTRODUCTION

After helping me arrange material for this book, my daughter Sarah remarked, "Just reading these quotes made me feel better."

Then, I realized that this was no ordinary reference book of collected quotations. It was also a source of inspiration and humor.

You may choose to use this book in several ways:

You could sit and read a section from start to finish as you would an ordinary book. Many quotes may tickle you because of the humor self-contained, or because they echo, contradict, or confirm other thoughts nearby.

Thumb through or open the book randomly, and read the first quote that pops up. It may be just what you need to hear at that moment.

Find a quote you are especially drawn to and savor it for an hour, a day, or a week. Allow it to provide affirmation and to help uplift some part of your life.

Also, use this book as you would any reference work. It can serve as a wonderful resource for writers, speakers, editors, clergy, teachers, salespeople, businesspeople, parents, and others who rely on the power of the written or spoken word.

No matter how you use *Quotations to Cheer You Up When the World Is Getting You Down,* I hope it enriches your life.

Allen Klein

Pleasant words are as an honeycomb, sweet to the soul, and
health to the bones.
Proverbs 16:24

amuse • amusing • amusement

a•muse *vt* to keep pleasantly or enjoyably occupied or interested: entertain

a•mus•ing *adj* entertaining; diverting

a•muse•ment *n* the condition or state of being amused

If you would rule the world quietly, you must keep it amused.
Ralph Waldo Emerson

The main obligation is to amuse yourself.
S. J. Perelman

When men are rightly occupied, their amusement grows out of their work, as the color-petals out of a fruitful flower.
John Ruskin

The art of medicine consists of amusing the patient while nature cures the disease.
Voltaire

Be amusing; never tell unkind stories; above all, never tell long ones.
Benjamin Disraeli

cheer • cheerful • chuckle
clown • comedian • comedy
comic • comical

cheer *n*   *1.* state of mind; feeling; spirit; mood   *2.* gladness; joy; gaiety; encouragement

cheer *vt*   *1.* to make happy or glad   *2.* to grow or be cheerful

cheer•ful *adj*   gay; joyful; full of cheer   **cheer•ful•ly** *adv*   **cheer•ful•ness** *n*

Be of good cheer.
William Shakespeare

While there is a chance of the world getting through its troubles, I hold that a reasonable man has to behave as though he were sure of it. If at the end your cheerfulness is not justified, at any rate you will have been cheerful.
H. G. Wells

Fake feeling good. . . . You're going to have to learn to fake cheerfulness. Believe it or not, eventually that effort will pay off: you'll actually start feeling happier.
Jean Bach

I can't be happy every day but I can be cheerful.
Beverly Sills

Cheerfulness keeps up a kind of daylight in the mind, and fills it with a steady and perpetual serenity.
Joseph Addison

A glad heart makes a cheerful countenance . . . a cheerful heart has a continual feast.
Proverbs 15:13–15

Since God has given me a cheerful heart, He will forgive me for serving Him cheerfully.
Franz Joseph Haydn

Nothing is more beautiful than cheerfulness in an old face.
Jean Paul Richter

A happy woman is one who has no cares at all; a cheerful woman is one who has cares but doesn't let them get her down.
Beverly Sills

Cheerfulness is like money well expended in charity; the more we dispense of it, the greater our possession.
Victor Hugo

The best way to cheer yourself is to try to cheer somebody else up.
Mark Twain

chuck•le *vi* to laugh in mild amusement, softly in a low tone

---

A chuckle a day may not keep the doctor away, but it sure does make those times in life's waiting room a little more bearable.
Anne Wilson Schaef

clown *n*   a person who plays the fool, invents jokes or pranks; a buffoon

---

A clown is like aspirin, only he works twice as fast.
Groucho Marx

Though the clown is often deadpan, he is a connoisseur of laughter.
Mel Gussow

A clown sees life simply, without complications.
George Bishop

A clown is a poet in action.
Henry Miller

A good clown caricatures his fellow men; a great one parodies himself.
Pierre Mariel

It is meat and drink to me to see a clown.
William Shakespeare

The arrival of a good clown exercises a more beneficial influence upon the health of a town than of twenty asses laden with drugs.
Thomas Sydenham

The comic spirit masquerades in all things we say and do. We are each a clown and do not need to put on a white face.
James Hillman

Clowns are ordinary folk, jest like you and me, only worse.
Edward Fitchner

I remain just one thing and one thing only, and that is a clown. It places me on a far higher plane than any politician.
Charlie Chaplin

The art of the clown is more profound than we think. . . . It is the comic mirror of tragedy and the tragic mirror of comedy.
André Suarès

Clown and guru are a single identity: the satiric and sublime side of the same higher vision of life.
Theodore Rozak

Send in the clowns.
Stephen Sondheim

co·me·di·an *n*   one who plays comic parts

com·e·dy *n*   the humorous element in life or in a literary work; an amusing event or events

com·ic *adj*   having to do with comedy; intended to be humorous, funny, amusing   **com·ic** *n*

com·i·cal *adj* causing laughter because of humor unexpectedly introduced   **com·i·cal·it·y** *n* **com·i·cal·ly** *adv*

Professor to student: "Ask me what is the secret of comedy."
Student: "What is the secret . . . ?"
Professor: "Timing!"
Anonymous

Comedy has to be truth. You take the truth and put a little curlicue at the end.
Sid Caesar

Comedy breaks down walls.
Goldie Hawn

Any kind of comedy releases, you know, frustration.
Andrew Dice Clay

Comedy, like sodomy, is an unnatural act.
Marty Feldman

Comedy is relief.
Sid Caesar

Comedy is allied to justice.
Aristophanes

Comedy is a mysterious and unexplored art.
Robert Klein

Comedy is essentially a miracle. I believe I'm as important to society as a doctor; to create laughter creates magic. These days nothing is more important.
Kathleen Freeman

Comedy is the art of making people laugh without making them puke.
Steve Martin

Most comics make jokes to defend themselves against what they see as a hostile and inhumane world . . . often a deeply felt rage.
Samuel S. Janus

Comedy is a socially acceptable form of hostility and aggression. That is what comics do, stand the world upside down.
George Carlin

Stand-up comedy is the art of letting an audience laugh by simulating spontaneity.
Lee Glickstein

Comedy is an escape, not from truth but from despair; a narrow escape into faith.
Christopher Fry

Comedy is in my blood. Frankly, I wish it were in my act!
Rodney Dangerfield

They don't seem to write . . . comedy anymore—just a series of gags.
Barbara Stanwyck

In all comedy there is something regressive that takes us back to the world of play that we first knew as children.
Roger Polhemus

Comedy is mentally pulling the rug out from under each person in your audience. But first, you have to get them to stand on it. You have to fool them, because if they see you preparing to tug on the rug, they'll move.
Gene Perret

Comedy is an ability to observe and see what's funny in a situation and be able to forget yourself enough to do it.
Madeline Kahn

A comedian is not a man who says funny things. A comedian is one who says things funny.
Ed Wynn

Harpo Marx looks like a musical comedy.
Walter Kerr

The whole object of comedy is to be yourself and the closer you get to that, the funnier you will be.
Jerry Seinfeld

To listen to your own silence is the key to comedy.
Elayne Boosler

Science opens to us the book of nature; comedy, the book of human nature.
Anonymous

What kills comedy is being too close to something, being too narrow-minded.
Gene Perret

You've got to realize when all goes well, and everything is beautiful, you have no comedy. It's when somebody steps on the bride's train or belches during the ceremony, then you've got comedy.
Phyllis Diller

I call my stuff three-day comedy. First they laugh, and three days later they go, "Oh, God, this is what she was talking about."
Roseanne Barr

Comedy is simply a funny way of being serious.
Peter Ustinov

The only way to get a serious message across is through comedy.
Woody Harrelson

Comic vision often leads to serious solutions.
Malcolm L. Kushner

Comedy is the main weapon we have against "The Horror." With it we can strike a blow at death itself. Or, at least, poke a hole in the pretentious notion that there is something dignified about it.
John Callahan

Pointing out the comic elements of a situation can bring a sense of proportion and perspective to what might otherwise seem an overwhelming problem.
Harvey Mindess

The most protean aspect of comedy is its potentiality for transcending itself, for responding to the conditions of tragedy by laughing in the darkness.
Harry Levin

To tragedy belongs guilt and judgment; to comedy, love and grace.
Conrad Hyers

The comic, more than the tragic, because it ignites hope, leads to more, not less, participation in the struggle for a just world.
Harvey Cox

Comedy is never so comic as when the comedian teeters on the edge of death.
Robert Payne

Dying is easy, comedy is hard.
Edmund Gwenn

You can make comedy about anything—death, war, cancer. You just have to be twice as good.
Robert Klein

Tragedy and comedy are but two aspects of what is real, and whether we see the tragic or the humorous is a matter of perspective.
Dr. Arnold Beisser

Life is a tragedy when seen in close-up, but a comedy in longshot.
Charlie Chaplin

The more one suffers, the more, I believe, one has a sense of the comic. It is only by the deepest suffering that one acquires the authority in the art of the comic.
Søren Kierkegaard

What a fine comedy this world would be if one did not play a part in it.
Denis Diderot

God writes a lot of comedy . . . the trouble is, he's stuck with so many bad actors who don't know how to play funny.
Garrison Keillor

Life literally abounds in comedy if you just look around you.
Mel Brooks

enjoy • enjoyment

en•joy *vt*   to experience with joy; relish; gain pleasure from

en•joy•ment *n*   the state or act of enjoying

There is no cure for birth or death save to enjoy the interval.
George Santayana

I'm all for rational enjoyment, and so forth, but I think a fellow makes himself conspicuous when he throws soft-boiled eggs at the electric fan.
P. G. Wodehouse

If you're going to do something wrong, at least enjoy it.
Leo Rosten

I believe the right question to ask, respecting all ornament, is simply this: Was it done with enjoyment—was the carver happy while he was about it?
John Ruskin

There are two things to aim at in life: first, to get what you want; and, after that, to enjoy it. Only the wisest of mankind achieve the second.
Logan Pearsall Smith

All of the animals, excepting man, know that the principal business of life is to enjoy it.
Samuel Butler

Enjoy today and don't waste it grieving over a bad yesterday—tomorrow may be even worse.
Anonymous

Enjoy yourself. These are the "good old days" you're going to miss in the years ahead.
Anonymous

Enjoyment is not a goal, it is a feeling that accompanies important ongoing activity.
Paul Goodman

Not what we have, but what we enjoy, constitutes our abundance.
Anonymous

No man is a failure who is enjoying life.
William Feather

The art of life is to know how to enjoy a little and to endure much.
William Hazlitt

Just because you're miserable doesn't mean you can't enjoy your life.
Annette Goodheart

Everyone only goes around the track once in life, and if you don't enjoy that trip, it's pretty pathetic.
Gary Rogers

Why not learn to enjoy the little things—there are so many of them.
Anonymous

A person will be called to account on Judgment Day for every permissible thing he might have enjoyed but did not.
Talmud

folly • fool • foolish
frivolity • frivolous
fun • funny

fol·ly *n*   lacking sense, understanding, or rational conduct; foolishness

---

A little folly now and then is cherished by the wisest of men.
Anonymous

A touch of folly is needed if we are to extricate ourselves
successfully from some of the hazards of life.
La Rochefoucauld

He who is aware of his folly is wise.
Yiddish proverb

The man who lives free from folly is not so wise as he thinks.
La Rochefoucauld

Folly is our constant companion throughout life. If someone
appears wise, it is only because his follies are suited to his age
and station.
La Rochefoucauld

The most exquisite folly is made of wisdom spun too fine.
Benjamin Franklin

A good folly is worth whatever you pay for it.
George Ade

It would be a great reform in politics if wisdom could be made to spread as easily and rapidly as folly.
Winston Churchill

The follies which a man regrets the most in his life are those which he didn't commit when he had the opportunity.
Helen Rowland

Come, let us give a little time to folly . . . and even in a melancholy day let us find time for an hour of pleasure.
Saint Bonaventura

fool *n*   a person with little judgment, common sense, or wisdom; silly person; simpleton

fool·ish *adj*   acting like a fool; being silly   **fool·ish·ness** *n*

———————————

Fools rush in where angels fear to tread.
Alexander Pope

Fools rush in—and get all the best seats.
Marybeth Weston

Lord, what fools these mortals be!
William Shakespeare

God watches over fools.
Yiddish proverb

Foolery, sir, does walk about the orb like the sun: it shines everywhere.
William Shakespeare

If every fool wore a crown, we should all be kings.
Welsh proverb

Ninety-nine percent of the people in the world are fools and the rest of us are in great danger of contagion.
Thornton Wilder

There are as many fools in the world as there are people.
Sigmund Freud

Let us be thankful for the fools. But for them the rest of us could not succeed.
Mark Twain

Aren't we all fools . . . in one or two things? . . . All the same, even a fool, though, can sometimes give good advice.
Martin Campbell Brockenhurst

There are things that even the wise fail to do, while the fool hits the point.
Zen saying

Get all the fools on your side and you can be elected to anything.
Frank Dane

Controversy equalizes fools and wise men—and the fools know it.
Oliver Wendell Holmes, Jr.

Wise men don't need advice. Fools don't take it.
Benjamin Franklin

Wise men talk because they have something to say; fools talk because they have to say something.
Plato

Why is it that fools always have the instinct to hunt out the unpleasant secrets of life, and the hardiness to mention them?
Emily Eden

I have great faith in fools; self-confidence my friends call it.
Edgar Allan Poe

Give me the young man who has brains enough to make a fool
of himself.
Robert Louis Stevenson

Real friends are those who upon watching you make a fool of yourself do not feel that the job was done permanently.
Anonymous

If any man among you seemeth to be wise in this world, let him become a fool, that he may be wise.
Corinthians I 3:18

If the fool would persist in his folly, he would become wise.
William Blake

There is a foolish corner in the brain of the wisest man.
Aristotle

Neither man nor woman can be worth anything until they have discovered that they are fools.
William Lamb, Viscount Melbourne

April 1. This is the day upon which we are reminded of what we are on the other three hundred and sixty-four.
Mark Twain

A fellow who is always declaring he's no fool usually has his suspicions.
Wilson Mizner

If I want to look at a fool, I have only to look in a mirror.
Seneca

Life is only a stage to play the fool upon as long as the part amuses us.
Robert Louis Stevenson

Almost all new ideas have a certain aspect of foolishness when they are first produced.
Alfred North Whitehead

I wasn't born a fool. It took work to get this way.
Danny Kaye

Without the fool's blunt observations and wise epigrams, our inner landscape might become a sterile wasteland.
Sallie Nichols

To never see a fool you lock yourself in your room and smash the looking-glass.
Carl Sandburg

Go, teach eternal wisdom how to rule—
Then drop into thyself, and be a fool!
Alexander Pope

You must play the fool a little if you would not be thought wholly a fool.
Michel de Montaigne

When I was a little boy, I had but a little wit,
'Tis a long time ago, and I have no more yet;
Nor ever ever shall, until that I die,
For the longer I live the more fool am I.
Anonymous

There is no fool like an old fool.
John Lyly

There's no fool like an old fool—you can't beat experience.
Jacob M. Braude

Every man is a damn fool for at least five minutes every day;
wisdom consists of not exceeding that limit.
Elbert Hubbard

One fool at least in every married couple.
Henry Fielding

Foolishness, like charity, begins at home.
Harvey Mindess

One has often known many a wise word to come from a mouth
reputed foolish; for that kind of madness, which uneducated and
stupid people call folly, really may mean inspiration.
Guillaume de la Pierre

The young man who has not wept is a savage, and the old man
who will not laugh is a fool.
George Santayana

It is better to be a fool than to be dead.
Robert Louis Stevenson

We must all learn to live together as brothers. Or we will all
perish together as fools.
Martin Luther King, Jr.

If it weren't for the brief respite we give the world with our
foolishness, the world would see mass suicide in numbers that
compare favorably with the death rate of the lemmings.
Groucho Marx

We have no choice, to be a human being is to be a latent fool.
The choice we have is whether or not we are going to be
practicing fools.
Stewart Emery

fri•vol•i•ty *n*   *1.* the quality or state of being frivolous   *2.* a frivolous act or thing

friv•o•lous *adj*   not serious or sensible; silly or light-minded; giddy

---

It is because they can be frivolous at times that the majority of people do not hang themselves.
Voltaire

Frivolity is almost, almost the definition of curiosity.
José Ortega y Gasset

fun *n* *1.* a) liveliness or playful; amusement, recreation, sport; b) enjoyment or pleasure *2.* a source of merriment

fun•ny *adj* causing laughter or amusement; humorous; laughable

---

I think of life itself now as a wonderful play that I've written for myself . . . and so my purpose is to have the utmost fun playing my part.
Shirley MacLaine

It is more important to have fun than it is to be funny.
Laurence J. Peter

Being funny is not one thing. Funniness can—and does—take a thousand and one forms.
Steve Allen

An amateur thinks it's funny if you dress a man up as an old lady, put him in a wheelchair, and give the wheelchair a push that sends it spinning down a slope towards a stone wall. For a pro, it's got to be a real old lady.
Groucho Marx

To a certain extent colds, baldness, mild allergies, hernias, toothaches, bunions, boils, and pimples are funny.
Paul Dickson

Words with a *k* in them are funny. If it doesn't have a *k*, it's not funny.
Neil Simon

An egg is funny, an orange is not!
Fred Allen

I have read many books by alleged experts, explaining the basis of humor and attempting to describe what is funny and what isn't. I doubt if any comedian can honestly say why he is funny and why his next-door neighbor is not.
Groucho Marx

It could be that if I were not afraid to just "be me" I would be naturally funny.
Hugh Prather

Here's my advice: Go ahead and be whacky. Get into a crazy frame of mind and ask what's funny about what you're doing.
Roger von Oech

I guess I like to have fun.
Madonna

Fun is fun but no girl wants to laugh all of the time.
Anita Loos

It's hard to be funny when you have to be clean.
Mae West

Whether it is fun to go to bed with a good book depends a great deal on who's reading it.
Kenneth Patchen

Some tickling or telling funny stories in bed can make sex more interesting.
"Dr. Ruth" Westheimer

I rhyme for fun.
Robert Burns

Golf is the most fun you can have without taking your clothes off.
Chi Chi Rodriguez

Have fun! Misery is optional.
Jean Westcott

A company that has fun, where employees lunch with each other, put cartoons on the wall and celebrate, is spirited, creative and usually profitable.
David Baum

Most of the time I don't have any fun. The rest of the time I don't have any fun at all.
Woody Allen

From there to here, and here to there, funny things are everywhere.
Dr. Seuss

If you're going to make fun of someone, start with yourself.
Paul Dickson

Man may often be funniest when he least means to be.
Carlo Weber

Life is a combination of comedy and tragedy. Some of the funniest things I've ever heard were said at funerals.
Shirley MacLaine

A spirit of fun should pervade every meeting because it helps people participate and learn.
Gene Perret

If it's not fun, you're not doing it right.
Bob Basso

People who can agree on what's funny can usually agree on other things.
Anonymous

Give us, Lord,
A bit of sun,
A bit of work,
And a bit of fun.
English prayer

Work is much more fun than fun.
Noel Coward

The only way the magic works is by hard work. But hard work
can be fun.
Jim Henson

Anything worth taking seriously is worth making fun of.
Tom Lehrer

Being "funny" doesn't mean you aren't serious.
Gene Shalit

What is funny about us is precisely that we take ourselves too
seriously.
Reinhold Niebuhr

One of the best things people can have up their sleeves is a funny bone.
Richard L. Weaver II

Nothing lives on so fresh and evergreen as the love with a funny bone.
George Jean Nathan

Once you have them by the funny bone, their hearts and minds will follow.
Robert Wieder

You can't really be strong until you see a funny side to things.
Ken Kesey

Life does not cease to be funny when people die any more than it ceases to be serious when people laugh.
George Bernard Shaw

This is what it's all about: If you can't have fun at it, there's no sense hanging around.
Joe Montana

In this job, you have only two choices: you are either funny deliberately or you are funny unintentionally.
Henry Kissinger

Have fun . . . Anything can change, without warning, and that's why I try not to take any of what's happened too seriously.
Donald Trump

To love what you do and feel that it matters—how could anything be more fun?
Katharine Graham

Are we having fun yet?
Carol Burnett

grin

grin *vi* to smile broadly in pleasure, amusement, or foolish embarrassment **grin** *n*

Care to our coffin adds a nail, no doubt,
And every grin so merry draws one out.
John Wolcot

Grin when you bare it—it's the only way.
Dolly Parton

All nature wears one universal grin.
Henry Fielding

happy • happiness
hope • hopeful
humor • humorist • humorous

hap·py *adj* a feeling of great pleasure, contentment, joy; glad; pleased

hap·pi·ness *n* *1.* a state of contentment and well-being *2.* pleasurable satisfaction *3.* felicity

---

The right to happiness is fundamental.
Bertolt Brecht

There is no duty we so much underrate as the duty of being happy.
Robert Louis Stevenson

We hold these truths to be self-evident, that all men are created equal, that they are endowed by their Creator with certain unalienable rights, that among these are life, liberty, and the pursuit of happiness.
Declaration of Independence

The Constitution only guarantees the American people the right to pursue happiness. You have to catch it yourself.
Benjamin Franklin

Happiness is a warm puppy.
Charles Schulz

We have lived through the era when happiness was a warm
puppy, and the era when happiness was a dry martini, and now
we have come to the era when happiness is "knowing what
your uterus looks like."
Nora Ephron

Happiness is like a cat. If you try to coax it or call it, it will
avoid you. It will never come. But if you pay no attention to it
and go about your business, you'll find it rubbing against your
legs and jumping into your lap.
William Bennett

Happy as a fish in water.
Victor Cherbuliez

Happy as a king.
John Gay

Happy as a June bug.
Anonymous

Happiness is the sublime moment when you get out of your corsets at night.
Joyce Grenfell

All happiness depends on a leisurely breakfast.
John Gunther

Happiness is a Chinese meal; sorrow is a nourishment forever.
Carolyn Kizer

Happiness? A good cigar, a good meal, a good cigar and a good woman—or a bad woman; it depends on how much happiness you can handle.
George Burns

Happiness is a way station between too little and too much.
Channing Pollock

Happiness is no laughing matter.
Richard Whately

Happy as a child.
William Wordsworth

Happy is the child whose father died rich.
Proverb

Happiness is found in doing, not merely possessing.
Napoleon Hill

True happiness may be sought, thought, or caught—but never
bought.
Anonymous

Money can't buy happiness . . . But then, happiness can't buy
government-insured CD's.
David Addison
character from Moonlighting

Whoever said money can't buy happiness didn't know where to
shop.
Anonymous

Money can't buy happiness but it will get you a better class of
memories.
Ronald Reagan

The best way for a person to have happy thoughts is to count his blessings and not his cash.
Anonymous

It's pretty hard to tell what does bring happiness; poverty and wealth have both failed.
Kin Hubbard

When I was young, I used to think that wealth and power would bring me happiness . . . I was right.
Gahan Wilson

The happiness of life is made up of minute fractions—the little, soon-forgotten charities of a kiss or smile, a kind look or heartfelt compliment.
Samuel Taylor Coleridge

The world is so full of a number of things, I'm sure we should all be as happy as kings.
Robert Louis Stevenson

Happiness lies in the joy of achievement and the thrill of creative effort.
Franklin D. Roosevelt

Happiness lies in the fulfillment of the spirit through the body.
Cyril Connolly

Happiness is bumping into Raquel Welch . . . very slowly.
Laugh-In

Happiness is too many things these days for anyone to wish it on anyone lightly. So let's just wish each other a bileless New Year and leave it at that.
Judith Crist

Happiness is a very small desk and a very big wastebasket.
Robert Orben

Happiness is your dentist telling you it won't hurt and then having him catch his hand in the drill.
Johnny Carson

Happiness is having a large, loving, caring, close-knit family in another city.
George Burns

Make happy those who are near, and those who are far will come.
Chinese proverb

That action is best which procures the greatest happiness for the greatest numbers.
Francis Hutcheson

We all live with the objective of being happy: our lives are all different and yet the same.
Anne Frank

Happy people plan actions, they don't plan results.
Dennis Wholey

The really happy man is one who can enjoy the scenery on a detour.
Anonymous

If you would be happy for a week, take a wife; if you would be happy for a month, kill a pig; but if you would be happy all your life, plant a garden.
Chinese proverb

Happiness depends upon ourselves.
Aristotle

I am kind of a paranoiac in reverse. I suspect people of plotting
to make me happy.
J. D. Salinger

Most folks are about as happy as they make up their minds
to be.
Abraham Lincoln

It is not the level of prosperity that makes for happiness but the
kinship of heart to heart and the way we look at the world. Both
attitudes are within our power, so that a man is happy so long as
he chooses to be happy, and no one can stop him.
Aleksandr Solzhenitsyn

You are much happier when you are happy than when you ain't.
Ogden Nash

When I'm happy I feel like crying, but when I'm sad I don't feel like laughing. I think it's better to be happy. Then you get two feelings for the price of one.
Lily Tomlin as Edith Ann

A man's happiness or unhappiness depends as much on his temperament as on his destiny.
La Rochefoucauld

Do you prefer that you be right or happy?
A Course in Miracles

Happiness comes most to persons who seek it least, and think least about it. It is not an object to be sought, it is a state to be induced. It must follow and not lead. It must overtake you, and not you overtake it.
John Burroughs

The search for happiness is one of the chief sources of unhappiness.
Eric Hoffer

If only we'd stop trying to be happy we could have a pretty good time.
Edith Wharton

The greatest happiness you can have is knowing that you do not necessarily require happiness.
William Saroyan

Most people ask for happiness on condition. Happiness can only be felt if you don't set any condition.
Arthur Rubinstein

We always have enough to be happy if we are enjoying what we do have—and not worrying about what we don't have.
Ken Keyes, Jr.

When one door of happiness closes, another opens, but often we look so long at the closed door that we do not see the one that has been opened for us.
Helen Keller

Happiness sneaks in through a door you didn't know you left open.
John Barrymore

If you ever find happiness by hunting for it, you will find it, as the old woman did her lost spectacles, safe on her own nose all the time.
Josh Billings

(Happiness) always looks small while you hold it in your hands, but let it go, and you learn at once how big and precious it is.
Maksim Gorky

Happiness makes up in height for what it lacks in length.
Robert Frost

Happiness is a butterfly, which, when pursued, is always just beyond your grasp, but which, if you will sit down quietly, may alight upon you.
Nathaniel Hawthorne

To be busy is man's only happiness.
Mark Twain

The only way to avoid being miserable is not to have enough leisure to wonder whether you are happy or not.
George Bernard Shaw

We act as though comfort and luxury were the chief requirements of life, when all that we need to make us really happy is something to be enthusiastic about.
Charles Kingsley

One thing I know: the only ones among you who will be really happy are those who will have sought and found how to serve.
Albert Schweitzer

There is no happiness except in the realization that we have accomplished something.
Henry Ford

For the happiest life, days should be rigorously planned, nights left open to chance.
Mignon McLaughlin

In order to be utterly happy the only thing necessary is to refrain from comparing this moment with other moments in the past, which I often did not fully enjoy because I was comparing them with other moments of the future.
André Gide

People don't notice whether it's winter or summer when they're happy.
Anton Chekhov

One of the things I keep learning is that the secret of being happy is doing things for other people.
Dick Gregory

Make one person happy each day and in forty years you will have made 14,600 human beings happy for a little time at least.
Charley Willey

You are forgiven for your happiness and your successes only if you generously consent to share them.
Albert Camus

When someone does something good, applaud! You will make
two people happy.
Samuel Goldwyn

Happiness consists of living each day as if it were the first day of
your honeymoon and the last day of your vacation.
Anonymous

A happy marriage is a long conversation which always seems
too short.
André Maurois

The husband who wants a happy marriage should learn to keep
his mouth shut and his checkbook open.
Groucho Marx

He is the happiest, be he king or peasant, who finds peace
in his home.
Goethe

Never fear spoiling children by making them too happy.
Happiness is the atmosphere in which all good affections grow.
Ann Eliza Bray

It's never too late to have a happy childhood.
Anonymous

"Did you have a happy childhood?" is a false question. As a child I did not know what happiness was, and whether I was happy or not. I was too busy being.
Alistair Reid

The supreme happiness of life is the conviction that we are loved.
Victor Hugo

[In the Orient people believed] that the basis of all disease was unhappiness. Thus to make a patient happy again was to restore him to health.
Donald Law

The simple truth is that happy people generally don't get sick.
Dr. Bernie Siegel

Every minute your mouth is turned down you lose sixty seconds of happiness.
Tom Walsh

If happiness truly consisted in physical ease and freedom from care, then the happiest individual would not be either a man or a woman; [but] an American cow.
William Lyon Phelps

Part of the happiness of life consists not in fighting battles but in avoiding them. A masterly retreat is in itself a victory.
Norman Vincent Peale

If you want others to be happy, practice compassion. If you want to be happy, practice compassion.
Dalai Lama

If there were in the world today any large number of people who desired their own happiness more than they desired the unhappiness of others, we could have a paradise in a few years.
Bertrand Russell

Happiness is when what you think, what you say, and what you do are in harmony.
Mahatma Gandhi

Worry doesn't help tomorrow's troubles, but it does ruin today's happiness.
Anonymous

Suffering is not a prerequisite for happiness.
Judy Tatelbaum

Talk happiness. The world is sad enough
Without your woe. No path is wholly rough.
Ella Wheeler Wilcox

To love is to suffer. To avoid suffering one must not love. But then one suffers from not loving. Therefore, to love is to suffer, not to love is to suffer, to suffer is to suffer. To be happy is to love. To be happy then is to suffer. But suffering makes one unhappy. Therefore to be unhappy one must love or love to suffer. Or suffer from too much happiness.
Woody Allen

There is only one way to happiness and that is to cease worrying about things which are beyond the power of our will.
Epictetus

Human life is basically a comedy. Even its tragedies often seem comic to the spectator, and not infrequently they actually have comic touches to the victim. Happiness probably consists largely in the capacity to detect and relish them.

H. L. Mencken

If God told you exactly what it was you were to do, you would be happy doing it no matter what it was. What you're doing is what God wants you to do. Be happy.

Werner Erhard

People who postpone happiness are like children who try chasing rainbows in an effort to find the pot of gold at the rainbow's end. . . . Your life will never be fulfilled until you are happy here and now.

Ken Keyes, Jr.

Don't worry, be happy.
Meher Baba
(popularized by Bobby McFerrin)

May all beings be happy.
Zen saying

hope *n*   a feeling something desired will happen or be received; expectation accompanied by a wish

hope *v*   to desire with expectation of fulfillment

hope•ful *adj*   feeling hope; expecting to get what one wishes

———————

The important thing is not that we can live on hope alone, but that life is not worth living without it.
Harvey Milk

Hold your head high, stick your chest out. You can make it. It gets dark sometimes but morning comes . . . Keep hope alive.
Jesse Jackson

A leader is a dealer in hope.
Napoleon Bonaparte

Great hopes make great men.
Thomas Fuller

True hope is swift, and flies with swallow's wings;
Kings it makes gods, and meaner creatures kings.
William Shakespeare

Hope for miracles, but don't rely on one.
Yiddish proverb

Hope is the feeling you have that the feeling you have isn't
permanent.
Jean Kerr

There are no hopeless situations; there are only men who have
grown hopeless about them.
Clare Boothe Luce

There is no medicine like hope, no incentive so great, and no
tonic so powerful as expectation of something tomorrow.
O. S. Marden

Hope, like the gleaming taper's light,
Adorns and cheers our way;
And still, as darker grows the night,
Emits a brighter ray.
Oliver Goldsmith

Our hopes, often though they deceive us, lead us pleasantly
along the path of life.
La Rochefoucauld

There is hope for any man who can look in a mirror and laugh
at what he sees.
Anonymous

We charge our image-makers with assuming a tragic model for
society, whereas the comic model contains man's only hope.
Joseph C. McLelland

Hope springs eternal in the human breast.
Alexander Pope

Faith, hope, and charity—if you had more of the first two we'd
need less of the last.
Anonymous

Hope is the pillar that holds up the world. Hope is the dream of a waking man.
Pliny the Elder

Hope: Tomorrow's veneer over today's disappointment.
Evan Esar

Hope sees the invisible, feels the intangible and achieves the impossible.
Anonymous

Hope is necessary in every condition. The miseries of poverty, sickness, of captivity, would, without this comfort, be insupportable.
Samuel Johnson

Strong hope is a much greater stimulant of life than any single realized joy could be.
Friedrich Wilhelm Nietzsche

If it were not for hope, the heart would break.
Anonymous

Hope itself is a species of happiness, and perhaps the chief happiness which this world affords.
Samuel Johnson

Hope is a light diet, but very stimulating.
Honoré de Balzac

Cast your bread upon the waters, hoping it will be returned to you toasted and buttered.
Anonymous

hu·mor *n*   *1. a)* one's disposition or temperament   *b)* a mood or state of mind   *2.* whim; caprice; fancy   *3.* the quality that makes something amusing, funny, or ludicrous; comicality

hu·mor·ist *n*   a person noted for humor

hu·mor·ous *adj*   expressing humor; comical; funny

After God created the world, He made man and woman. Then, to keep the whole thing from collapsing, He invented humor.
Mack McGinnis

Humor is an affirmation of dignity, a declaration of man's superiority to all that befalls him.
Romain Gary

Humor results when society says you can't scratch certain things in public, but they itch in public.
Tom Walsh

A sense of humor can help you overlook the unattractive, tolerate the unpleasant, cope with the unexpected, and smile through the unbearable.
Moshe Waldoks

Humor is the healthy way of feeling "distance" between one's self and the problem, a way of standing off and looking at one's problems with perspective.
Rollo May

A sense of humor judges one's actions and the actions of others from a wider reference and a longer view and finds them incongruous. It dampens enthusiasm; it mocks hope; it pardons shortcomings; it consoles failure. It recommends moderation.
Thornton Wilder

Humor is a rich and versatile source of power—a spiritual resource very like prayer.
Marilyn R. Chandler

Humor is not a trick, not jokes. Humor is a presence in the world—like grace—and shines on everybody.
Garrison Keillor

A sense of humor is a gift from God, but like any gift, it can be abused.
Cal Samra

If humor is something like a sword, maybe it has to be strapped on, but nobody should go around without it in any period of time. . . . Since one of its chief constituents is taste, it should be used sparingly sometimes and left in its sheath at other times, but it should always be handy.
James Thurber

Humor is mankind's greatest blessing.
Mark Twain

With humor, as with practically everything else in life, moderation is usually the key. Relax, don't push.
Steve Allen

A cardinal rule of humor: Never say anything about anyone that the person can't change in five seconds. Use the AT&T test for stories and jokes—make sure it's *A*ppropriate, *T*imely and *T*asteful.
Susan RoAne

There are three rules for creating humor, but unfortunately no one knows what they are.
Laurence J. Peter

Be strong, believe in freedom and in God, love yourself, understand your sexuality, have a sense of humor, masturbate, don't judge people by their religion, color or sexual habits, love life and your family.
Madonna

Exaggerate a little. A tall tale in the service of humor is a noble thing indeed.
David Garfinkel

Humor is reason gone mad.
Groucho Marx

I don't know what humor is.
Will Rogers

All I know about humor is that I don't know anything about it.
Fred Allen

In matters of humor, what is appealing to one person is appalling to another.
Melvin Helitzer

One odd thing about humor is that it is almost impossible to write about it in a humorous way. The magic of the thing disappears under analysis and one is left with a puff of dry dust.
Steve Allen

Humor is the ability to see three sides of one coin.
Ned Rorem

Humor is emotional chaos remembered in tranquility.
James Thurber

Humor is a reminder that no matter how high the throne one sits on, one sits on one's bottom.
Taki

Humor may be defined as the kindly contemplation of the incongruities of life, and the artistic expression thereof.
Stephen Leacock

Humor can be dissected as a frog can, but the thing dies in the process and the innards are discouraging to any but the pure scientist.
E. B. White

I think I could grow a new tooth by next Thursday easier than I can define humor.
Grady Nutt

Defining and analyzing humor is a pastime of humorless people.
Robert Benchley

I deeply believe in humor—I don't believe in jokes.
Tom Peters

Gags die, humor doesn't.
Jack Benny

A sense of humor means looking at things from an offbeat angle.
Malcolm L. Kushner

Humor, like history and married women, repeats itself, and like well-bred detectives it assumes many disguises.
Stuart W. Knight

I see humor as food. I don't think that the only time people should eat food is when they're ill. An adequate share of humor and laughter represent an essential part of the diet of the healthy person.
Norman Cousins

Humor can be the appetizer or dessert, sometimes the main course, but not the whole meal or steady diet. No one wants cake all the time, or even steak.
Virginia Tooper

Humor is not a condiment; it's a main course. It's not a trinket; it's a gem. It doesn't need justification; it's essential.
Gene Perret

Humor is the great thing, the saving thing, after all. The minute it crops up, all our hardnesses yield, all our irritations and resentments flit away, and a sunny spirit takes their place.
Mark Twain

Like a welcome summer rain, humor may suddenly cleanse and cool the earth, the air and you.
Langston Hughes

I never had a sense of humor. What started me in a theatrical direction was finding at a very early age that I had a talent. I could impersonate chickens. Buk buk buk bacagh.
Jonathan Miller

I realize that humor isn't for everyone. It's only for people who want to have fun, enjoy life, and feel alive.
Anne Wilson Schaef

We're only young once, but with humor, we can be immature forever.
Art Gliner

A man will confess to treason, murder, arson, false teeth, or a wig. How many of them will own up to a lack of humor?
Frank Moore Colby

Imagination was given to us to compensate for what we are not; a sense of humor was provided to console us for what we are.
Mack McGinnis

Humor is a serious thing. I like to think of it as one of our greatest earliest natural resources, which must be preserved at all cost.
James Thurber

Humor can be serious. What it can't be is solemn.
John Cleese

There are two insults no human being will endure: that he has no sense of humor, and that he has never known trouble.
Sinclair Lewis

A person without a sense of humor is like a wagon without springs—jolted by every pebble in the road.
Henry Ward Beecher

In order to cultivate our sense of humor, we must thrive on change. We must learn to accept life and to accept ourselves . . . with a shrug and a smile . . . because it's all we've got.
Harvey Mindess

When the average person feels no one is in control, zany humor takes over.
Robert Orben

One doesn't have a sense of humor. It has you.
Larry Gelbart

God is a humorist. If you have any doubts about it, look in the mirror.
Ken Olson

Humor is laughing at what you haven't got when you ought to have it.
Romain Gary

Humor prevents a "hardening of the attitudes."
Joel Goodman

Nothing is better than the unintended humor of reality.
Steve Allen

Humor is an attitude. It's a way of looking at life and of telling others how you feel about what's happening around you.
Gene Perret

Good humor is the health of the soul, sadness its poison.
I. V. Stanislaus

Humor opposes directly those emotions which have been specifically recorded as being associated with precipitation of heart attack. These emotions are fear and rage. Humor acts to relieve fear. Rage is impossible when mirth prevails.
Dr. William F. Fry, Jr.

I think we're finally at a point where we've learned to see death with a sense of humor.
Katharine Hepburn

With humor death is less of a grave matter.
Glenn Vernon

Humor prevents one from becoming a tragic figure even though he/she is involved in tragic events.
E. T. "Cy" Eberhart

This I conceive to be the chemical function of humor: to change the character of our thought.
Lin Yutang

Warning: Humor may be hazardous to your illness.
Ellie Katz

Cancer is probably the most unfunny thing in the world, but I'm a comedienne, and even cancer couldn't stop me from seeing humor in what I went through.
Gilda Radner

Humor does not diminish the pain—it makes the space around it get bigger.
Allen Klein

Humor is tragedy plus time.
Mark Twain

Humor is the instinct for taking pain playfully.
Max Eastman

The secret source of humor is not joy but sorrow.
Mark Twain

Humor is a means of obtaining pleasure in spite of the
distressing effects that interface with it.
Sigmund Freud

Total absence of humor renders life impossible.
Colette

If I had no sense of humor, I should long ago have committed
suicide.
Mahatma Gandhi

Optimism and humor are the grease and glue of life. Without
both of them we would never have survived our captivity.
Philip Butler, Vietnam POW

I say it's time to take humor out of the closet. Change the
workplace motto from ''Grim and Bear It'' to
''Grin and Share It.''
Sheila Feigelson

Humor is as highly serious and specialized a job as shoeing a mule, and darned near as dangerous if you flub it.
Oren Arnold

Humor is falling downstairs if you do it while in the act of warning your wife not to.
Kenneth Bird

Humor is really laughing off a hurt, grinning at misery.
Bill Mauldin

Humor is just another defense against the universe.
Mel Brooks

Against the assault of humor, nothing can stand.
Mark Twain

Humor is a good way to tamp . . . the level of nastiness and violence in the world. We really ought to take humor more seriously.
Jeffrey Keefe

Humor offers an alternative to violence. . . . Humor gives us a choice.
Dr. William F. Fry, Jr.

Humor has a way of bringing people together. It unites people. In fact, I'm rather serious when I suggest that someone should plant a few whoopee cushions in the United Nations.
Ron Dentinger

We all need a sense of humor or someday we will wake up with no sense at all.
Melvin Helitzer

Fortune and humor govern the world.
La Rochefoucauld

When humor goes, there goes civilization.
Erma Bombeck

It has always surprised me how little attention philosophers have paid to humor, since it is a more significant process of mind than reason. Reason can only sort out perceptions, but the humor process is involved in changing them.
Edward de Bono

Here in America we have an immensely humorous people in a land of milk and honey and wit, who cherish the ideal of the "sense" of humor and at the same time are highly suspicious of anything that is non-serious.
E. B. White

Good humor may be said to be one of the very best articles of dress one can wear in society.
William Thackeray

A sense of humor is part of the art of leadership, of getting along with people, of getting things done.
Dwight D. Eisenhower

Any man who has had the job I've had and didn't have a sense of humor wouldn't still be here.
Harry Truman

Humor is my sword and my shield. It protects me. You can open a door with humor and drive a truck right through.
Alan Simpson

Managing to have a sense of humor makes it a lot easier to manage people.
Steve Wilson

If a presidential candidate is lacking in humor, don't vote for him.
Peggy Noonan

I think the next best thing to solving a problem is finding some humor in it.
Frank A. Clark

There is a close relationship between the "ha-ha" of humor and the "aha!" of discovery.
Roger von Oech

Good humor isn't a trait of character; it is an art which requires practice.
David Seabury

Learning humor is like learning math—practice makes perfect.
Jim Pelley

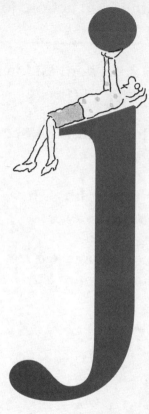

jest • joke
joy • joyful • joyfulness

jest *n*   a gay mood or lighthearted action; joking; fun   **jest** *v*

There's many a true word said in jest.
Anonymous

Good jests bite like lambs, not like dogs.
Anonymous

Jest for the health of it.
Patty Wooten

No sense of humor; jest lag.
Quote Magazine *(January 1, 1986)*

joke *n*   *1.* something done or said to arouse laughter   *2.* a humorous element in a situation

joke *vi*   to tell jokes or kid around

Even the gods love jokes.
Plato

A joke that has to be explained is at its wit's end.
Anonymous

You throw a perfectly straight line at the audience and then, right at the end, you curve it. Good jokes do that.
Abe Burrows

A joke is not a thing but a process, a trick you play on the listener's mind. You start him off toward a plausible goal, and then by a sudden twist you land him nowhere at all or just where he didn't expect to go.
Max Eastman

Every joke is a tiny revolution.
George Orwell

A good joke is the one ultimate and sacred thing which cannot be criticized. Our relations with a good joke are direct and even divine relations.
G. K. Chesterton

My way of joking is to tell the truth. It's the funniest joke in the world.
George Bernard Shaw

The funniest joke of all is the absolute truth stated simply and gracefully.
Carl Reiner

He that jokes confesses.
Italian proverb

A person reveals his character by nothing so clearly as the joke he resents.
G. C. Lichtenberg

A good joke is not an invention, but a discovery.
E. H. Gombrich

If there is no malice in your heart, there can't be none in your jokes.
Will Rogers

If you want someone to laugh at your jokes, tell him he has a sense of humor.
Herbert V. Prochnow

A sense of humor . . . is the ability to understand a joke . . . and that joke is oneself.
Clifton Fadiman

The only truly safe and proper subject for a joke is oneself. Many a person who thought this privilege extended to his or her spouse, parent, or child, has lived—but not very long—to find out otherwise.
Judith "Miss Manners" Martin

The aim of a joke is not to degrade the human being but to remind him that he is already degraded.
George Orwell

If you are willing to make yourself the butt of a joke, you become one of the guys, a human being, and people are more willing to listen to what you have to say.
Larry Wilde

Joke with good reason, not to appear jesters, but to obtain some advantage.
Cicero

I don't make jokes. I just watch the government and report the facts.
Will Rogers

Jokes of the proper kind, properly told, can do more to enlighten questions of politics, philosophy, and literature than any number of dull arguments.
Isaac Asimov

Were it not for my little jokes, I could not bear the burdens of
this office.
Abraham Lincoln

There are things of deadly earnest that can only be safely mentioned under cover of a joke.
J. J. Procter

Joking about death—or anything else that oppresses us—makes it less frightening.
Allen Klein

It is requisite for the relaxation of the mind that we make use, from time to time, of playful deeds and jokes.
Thomas Aquinas

Practical jokes aren't.
Craig Whatley

Forgive, O Lord, my little jokes on Thee and I'll forgive Thy great big one on me.
Robert Frost

Eternity is a mere moment, just long enough for a joke.
Hermann Hesse

Life is a joke that's just begun.
W. S. Gilbert

Life is God's joke on us. It's our mission to figure out the punchline.
John Guarrine

Life itself is a paradox: both meaningful and meaningless, important and insignificant, a joke and a yoke.
Wes "Scoop" Nisker

We should tackle reality in a slightly joky way, otherwise we miss its point.
Lawrence Durrell

A humorist tells himself every morning, "I hope it's going to be a rough day." When things are going well, it's much harder to make the right jokes.
Alan Coren

The crisis of today is the joke of tomorrow.
H. G. Wells

If Adam came on earth again the only thing he would recognize would be the old jokes.
Thomas Robert Dewar

There's no such thing as an old joke, unless you've heard it before.
Steve Allen

There is no such thing as an old joke—if you dress it up with new clothes.
Joey Adams

Comedy never changes. There are only eight to nine formats of jokes. . . . Funny is funny.
Milton Berle

There is no reason why a joke should not be appreciated more than once. Imagine how little good music there would be if, for example, a conductor refused to play Beethoven's Fifth Symphony on the grounds that his audience might have heard it before.
A. J. Herbert

It is a good deed to forget a poor joke.
Brendan Bracken

If you can't remember a joke—don't dismember it.
Anonymous

Act as if you enjoy telling the joke, which suggests you know
how to do it.
Leo Rosten

Nothing improves a joke more than telling it to your employees.
James Thurber

A joke isn't a joke until someone laughs.
Michael Crawford

joy *n*   happiness; delight; great pleasure

joy•ful *adj*   expressing or feeling joy; causing happiness; glad   **joy•ful•ness** *n*

Make a joyful noise unto the Lord.
Psalms 100:1

To discover joy is to return to a state of oneness with the universe.
Peggy Jenkins

Joy is life realizing what its parent, the universe, God, if you wish, is, was always, and shall ever be—joy.
Robert Ellwood

A thing of beauty is a joy forever.
John Keats

A wise man sings his joys in the closet of his heart.
Tibullus

Joy is the flag you fly when the Prince of Peace is in residence within your heart.
Wilfred Peterson

The opportunities for enjoyment in your life are limitless. If you feel you are not experiencing enough joy, you have only yourself to blame.
David E. Bresler

The sun does not shine for a few trees and flowers, but for the wide world's joy.
Henry Ward Beecher

When you finally allow yourself to trust joy and embrace it, you will find you dance with everything.
Emmanuel

You have to sniff out joy, keep your nose to the joy trail.
Buffy Sainte-Marie

If you wear a rubber nose for a week, your life will be changed because you will get in touch with the joy you can bring to the world.
Dr. Hunter "Patch" Adams

You increase your joy by increasing the pure joy of others.
Torkom Saraydarian

If you do a good job for others, you heal yourself at the same time, because a dose of joy is a spiritual cure. It transcends all barriers.
Ed Sullivan

Life's only lasting joy comes in erasing the boundary line between "mine" and "yours."
Anonymous

There is no hope of joy except in human relations.
Antoine de Saint-Exupéry

The only obstacle to releasing joy is the unwillingness to express love for someone or something.
Arnold Patent

Without kindness there can be no true joy.
Thomas Carlyle

If you do not get joy out of this life, how can you expect to get any happiness out of the next?
Hasidic saying

If you don't look for beauty, you won't see it. If you don't seek joy, you won't find it.
Dr. Christian Hageseth

When you jump for joy, beware that no one moves the ground from beneath your feet.
Stanislaw Lec

Joy is not in things, it is in us.
Benjamin Franklin

Paradise is here or nowhere: you must take your joy with you or you will never find it.
O. S. Marden

Life itself cannot give you joy
Unless you really will it.
Life just gives you time and space—
It's up to you to fill it.
Chinese proverb

Your joy is your sorrow unmasked.
And the selfsame well from which your laughter rises was
oftentimes filled with your tears.
Kahlil Gibran

Joy and woe are woven fine,
A clothing for the soul divine.
William Blake

Life is difficult—filled with problems and pain—and when living
hurts, joy eases the strain.
Sol Gordon and Harold Brecher

Be willing to access joy in the face of adversity.
C. W. Metcalf

Joy is more divine than sorrow, for joy is bread and sorrow is medicine.
Henry Ward Beecher

Weeping may endure for a night, but joy cometh in the morning.
Psalms 30:5

There cannot be day without night, joy without sorrow, nor spring without winter.
Zula Bennington Greene

Grief can take care of itself, but to get the full value of a joy you must have somebody to divide it with.
Mark Twain

Shared joys make a friend, not shared sufferings.
Friedrich Wilhelm Nietzsche

Friendship redoubleth joys, and cutteth griefs in half.
Francis Bacon

A joy that's shared is a joy made double.
English proverb

The trick is not how much pain you feel—but how much joy you feel.
Erica Jong

One joy scatters a hundred griefs.
Chinese proverb

Joy is not the absence of suffering. It is the presence of God.
Robert Schuller

Joy is the serious business of Heaven.
C. S. Lewis

He who binds to himself a joy
Does the winged life destroy;
But he who kisses the joy as it flies
Lives in eternity's sunrise.
William Blake

I find my joy of living in the fierce and ruthless battles of life, and my pleasure comes from learning something.
August Strindberg

A wise teacher makes learning a joy.
Proverb

The surgeon must forbid anger, hatred, and sadness in the patient, and remind him that the body grows fat from joy, and thin from sadness.
Dr. Henri de Mondeville

The joyfulness of a man prolongeth his days.
Apocrypha, Ecclesiasticus 30:22

"Did you bring joy?"
"Did you find joy?"
Egyptian god Osiris asks the deceased

Life is a well of joy.
Friedrich Wilhelm Nietzsche

Joys are our wings.
Jean Paul Richter

"On with the dance, let joy be unconfined" is my motto, whether there's any dance to dance or any joy to unconfine.
Mark Twain

laugh • laughter • levity

laugh *vi*   *1.* to make the explosive vocal sounds and physical movements that express mirth, amusement, ridicule   *2.* to be amused   *3.* to feel joyous   **laugh** *n*

laugh•ter *n*   the action or sound of laughing

To every thing there is a season, and a time to every purpose under the heaven. A time to be born, and a time to die. . . . A time to weep, and a time to laugh.
Ecclesiastes 3:1–2, 4

Rumor has it among linguists and word-doctors that this word [*laughter*] derives from the Sanskrit *lokha,* which meant trying to belch while riding on the back of a yak in full flight.
Rick Bernardo

Life can be wildly tragic at times, and I've had my share. But whatever happens to you, you have to keep a slightly comic attitude. In the final analysis, you have got not to forget to laugh.
Katharine Hepburn

We are all here for a spell; get all the good laughs you can.
Will Rogers

I wake up laughing. Yes, I wake up in the morning, and there I am just laughing my head off.
Bruce Willis

I learned quickly that when I made others laugh, they liked me. This lesson I will never forget.
Art Buchwald

I found people looked better when they laughed.
Mort Sahl

There is nothing in the world like making people laugh.
Carol Burnett

It's an odd job, making decent people laugh.
Molière

If I get big laughs, I'm a comedian. If I get little laughs, I'm a humorist. If I get no laughs, I'm a singer.
George Burns

The person who can bring the spirit of laughter into a room is indeed blessed.
Bennett Cerf

You have asked me to share some of my personal experiences regarding the benefits of laughter. Not the least of them is a Mercedes in my garage and three children with straight teeth.
Erma Bombeck

I draw my material from things that happen to me, like parents, my school, marriage. Some of it's true, some of it isn't. I don't care which as long as it gets a laugh.
Woody Allen

Without laughter, life on our planet would be intolerable. So important is laughter that societies highly reward those who make a living by inducing laughter in others.
Steve Allen

A good laugh is like manure to a farmer—it doesn't do any good until you spread it around.
Anonymous

In the beginning God made a man and a woman and set them on earth. Then the man and woman looked at each other and burst out laughing.

African myth

Man is distinguished from all other creatures by the faculty of laughter.
Joseph Addison

Man is the only animal that laughs and has a state legislature.
Samuel Butler

Dogs laugh, but they laugh with their tails.
Max Eastman

Laugh, and the world laughs with you;
Weep, and you weep alone;
For the sad old earth must borrow its mirth,
It has trouble enough of its own.
Ella Wheeler Wilcox

Laugh and the world laughs with you. Cry and you get all wet.
Anonymous

Laugh and the world laughs with you. Snore and you sleep alone.
Anthony Burgess

A laugh is worth a hundred groans in any market.
Charles Lamb

Genuine laughter is the physical effect produced in the rational being by what suddenly strikes his immortal soul as being damned funny.
Hilaire Belloc

The stimulus of a laugh is an intellectual event, yet it quickly goes on to block out all else. There are only two other phenomena that so completely take over your awareness—the orgasm and the sneeze.
Howard Pollio

What soap is to the body, laughter is to the soul.
Yiddish proverb

Laughter is like changing a baby's diaper—it doesn't permanently solve any problems, but it makes things more acceptable for a while.
Anonymous

He had a broad face and a little round belly
That shook, when he laughed, like a bowl full of jelly.
Clement C. Moore

She had a penetrating sort of laugh. Rather like a train going into
a tunnel.
P. G. Wodehouse

His laughter tinkled among the teacups.
T. S. Eliot

The most wasted day of all is that on which we have not
laughed.
Sébastien Chamfort

Seven days without laughter makes one weak.
Joel Goodman

We don't stop laughing because we grow old; we grow old
because we stop laughing.
Anonymous

If you laugh a lot, when you get older your wrinkles will be in the right places.
Andrew Mason

If you don't have wrinkles, you haven't laughed enough.
Phyllis Diller

When we laugh, muscles are activated. When we stop laughing, these muscles relax. Since muscle tension magnifies pain, many people with arthritis, rheumatism and other painful conditions benefit greatly from a healthy dose of laughter.
Dr. William F. Fry, Jr.

Ten minutes of genuine belly laughter had an anesthetic effect and would give me at least two hours of pain-free sleep.
Norman Cousins

Laughter is a tranquilizer with no side effects.
Arnold Glasgow

Laughter is a form of internal jogging.
Norman Cousins

It is bad to suppress laughter. It goes back down and spreads your hips.
Fred Allen

The four leading ways of breaking tension are: taking drugs, meditating, exercising, and laughing your ham off.
Laurence J. Peter and Bill Dana

Genuine laughter is a vent of the soul, the nostrils of the heart, and it is just as necessary for health and happiness as spring water is for a trout.
Josh Billings

Laughter lets me relax. It's the equivalent of taking a deep breath, letting it out and saying, "This too will pass."
Odette Pollar

Laughter is an instant vacation.
Milton Berle

Something special happens when people laugh together over something genuinely funny, and not hurtful to anyone. It's like a magic rain that showers down feelings of comfort, safety and belonging to a group.
Mary Jane Belfie

The health of any organization is directly proportional to its ability to laugh at itself.
Bob Ross

If you can laugh together, you can work together.
Robert Orben

A person who belly-laughs doesn't bellyache.
Susan Thurman

Laughter is the shortest distance between two people.
Victor Borge

He deserves Paradise who makes his companions laugh.
Koran

Gentlemen, why don't you laugh? With the fearful strain that is upon me night and day, if I did not laugh, I should die. You need this medicine as much as I do.
Abraham Lincoln

If we can open your mind to laughter, we can slip in a little information.
Virginia Tooper

He who laughs most, learns best.
John Cleese

To get 'em listening, get 'em laughing.
Allen Klein

We should call every truth false which was not accompanied by at least one laugh.
Friedrich Wilhelm Nietzsche

If I can get you to laugh with me, you like me better, which makes you more open to my ideas. And if I can persuade you to laugh at the particular point I make, by laughing at it you acknowledge its truth.
John Cleese

As soon as you have made a thought, laugh at it.
Lao-tzu

To make mistakes is human; to stumble is commonplace; to be able to laugh at yourself is maturity.
William Arthur Ward

All of us have schnozzles . . . if not in our faces, then in our character, minds or habits. When we admit our schnozzles, instead of defending them, we begin to laugh, and the world laughs with us.
Jimmy Durante

Nobody says you must laugh, but a sense of humor can help you overlook the unattractive, tolerate the unpleasant, cope with the unexpected, and smile through the day.
Ann Landers

By being frequently in the company of children, we may learn to recapture the will to laugh and the art of laughing at will.
Julius Gordon

When the first baby laughed for the first time, his laugh broke into a million pieces, and they all went skipping about. That was the beginning of fairies.
J. M. Barrie

If you can't make it better, you can laugh at it.
Erma Bombeck

Since everything is but an apparition, perfect in being what it is, having nothing to do with good or bad, acceptance or rejection, one may well burst out in laughter.
Long Chen Pa

If you wish to glimpse inside a human soul and get to know a man, don't bother analyzing his ways of being silent, of talking, of weeping, of seeing how much he is moved by noble ideas; you will get better results if you just watch him laugh. If he laughs well, he's a good man.
Fyodor Dostoyevski

Nothing, no experience, good or bad, no belief, no cause, is in itself momentous enough to monopolize the whole of life to the exclusion of laughter.
Alfred North Whitehead

If a man cannot laugh, there is some mistake made in putting him together. And if he will not laugh, he warrants as much keeping away from as a bear trap when it is set.
Josh Billings

If I were given the opportunity to present a gift to the next generation, it would be the ability for each individual to learn to laugh at himself.
Charles Schulz

Life, love, and laughter—what priceless gifts to give our children.
Phyllis Campbell Dryden

Laugh at yourself first, before anybody else can.
Elsa Maxwell

Suffering makes you laugh, too.
Yiddish proverb

You can turn painful situations around through laughter. If you can find humor in anything—even poverty—you can survive it.
Bill Cosby

St. Theresa of Avila always looked for novices who knew how to laugh, eat, and sleep. She was sure that if they ate heartily they were healthy, if they slept well they were more likely free of serious sin, and if they laughed they had the necessary disposition to survive a difficult life.
Quote Magazine *(January 1, 1986)*

Perhaps I know best why it is man alone who laughs; he alone suffers so deeply that he had to invent laughter.
Friedrich Wilhelm Nietzsche

Even if there is nothing to laugh about, laugh on credit.
Anonymous

As long as we can choose to laugh, it means we affirm life.
Esther Blumenfeld and Lynn Alpern

There is a thin line that separates laughter and pain, comedy and tragedy, humor and hurt. And how do you know laughter if there is no pain to compare it with?
Erma Bombeck

Laughter need not be cut out of anything, since it improves everything.
James Thurber

When you're hungry, sing. When you're hurt, laugh.
Jewish saying

Laughter and tears are both responses to frustration and exhaustion . . . I myself prefer to laugh, since there is less cleaning up to do afterward.
Kurt Vonnegut, Jr.

I have seen what a laugh can do. It can transform almost unbearable tears into something bearable, even hopeful.
Bob Hope

If I have to cry, I think of my sex life. If I have to laugh, I think of my sex life.
Glenda Jackson

Laughter and orgasm are great bedfellows.
John Callahan

It's okay to laugh in the bedroom so long as you don't point.
Will Durst

When one has understanding, one should laugh; one should not weep.
Hsüeh-T'ou

Laughter can be heard farther than weeping.
Yiddish proverb

Man is the only animal that laughs and weeps; for he is the only animal that is struck with the difference between what things are and what they might have been.
William Hazlitt

Laughter acknowledges the coexistence of the divine and the human, of joy and sorrow, of laughter and tears.
Carlo Weber

For what, after all, is the laughter a good clown brings us but the giddiness that comes from suddenly seeing, as if from a cosmic viewpoint, the absurdity of what the mighty are up to. For that moment, we taste the sanity of divine madness, and become, for as long as the joke lasts, fools of God.

Theodore Rozak

There are three things which are real: God, human folly, and laughter. The first two are beyond our comprehension. So we must do what we can with the third.

John F. Kennedy

Time spent laughing is time spent with the gods.

Japanese saying

Laughter, of course, can be strained, cruel, artificial and merely habitual. . . . But where it is real, laughter is the voice of faith.

Harvey Cox

It is pleasing to the dear God whenever thou rejoicest or laughest from the bottom of thy heart.

Martin Luther

God is a comedian playing to an audience that is afraid to laugh.
Voltaire

God laughs, it seems, because God knows how it all turns out in
the end.
Harvey Cox

Laughter is God's hand on a troubled world.
Minnie Pearl

The human race has only one really effective weapon and that is
laughter.
Mark Twain

Laughter is a safe and civilized alternative to violence.
Dr. Martin Grotjahn

When people are laughing, they're generally not killing one
another.
Alan Alda

Though a humorist may bomb occasionally, it is still better to exchange humorists than bombs, because you can't fight when you're laughing.
Jim Boren

Barking dogs may occasionally bite, but laughing men hardly ever shoot!
Konrad Lorenz

In prehistoric times, mankind often had only two choices in crisis situations: fight or flee. In modern times, humor offers us a third alternative; fight, flee—or laugh.
Robert Orben

Man, when you lose your laugh, you lose your footing.
Ken Kesey

Laughter? Does anyone ever care about laughter? I mean real laughter—beyond joking, jeering, ridicule. Laughter—delight unbounded, delight delectable, delight of delights.
Milan Kundera

School is over,
Oh, what fun!
Lessons finished,
Play begun.
Who'll run fastest.
You or I?
Who'll laugh loudest?
Let us try.
Kate Greenaway

He laughs best who laughs last.
English proverb

He who laughs last . . . thinks slowest.
Bob Lockhart

He who laughs, lasts.
Mary Pettibone Poole

Laughter is contagious . . . start an epidemic.
Susan Thurman

To laugh often and much; to win respect of intelligent people and the affection of children . . . to leave the world a better place . . . to know even one life has breathed easier because you have lived. This is to have succeeded.
Ralph Waldo Emerson

lev•i•ty *n*   light or gay disposition, speech, or behavior

———————————

A little levity will save many a good heavy thing from sinking.
Samuel Butler

My method is to take the utmost trouble to find the right thing to say, and then to say it with the utmost levity.
George Bernard Shaw

Nothing like a little judicious levity.
Robert Louis Stevenson

merry • mirth • mirthfulness

mer•ry *adj* full of laughter and fun; lively and gay; cheerful

---

A man hath no better thing under the sun than to eat and to
drink and to be merry.
Ecclesiastes 8:15

Eat, drink, and be merry, for tomorrow we may diet.
Anonymous

The best doctors in the world are Dr. Diet, Dr. Quiet, and Dr.
Merryman.
Jonathan Swift

A merry heart goes all the day.
William Shakespeare

He that is of a merry heart has a continual feast.
Proverbs 15:15

Merry have we met, and merry have we been;
Merry let us part, and merry meet again;
With our merry sing-song, happy, gay, and free,
With a merry ding-dong, happy let us be!
English rhyme

mirth *n* joyfulness, merriment, or gaiety, esp. when accompanied by laughter

mirth·ful·ness *n* expressing or causing mirth or merriment

———————

Mirth is like a flash of lightning that breaks through a gloom of clouds and glitters for a moment.
Joseph Addison

Mirth, and even cheerfulness, when employed as remedies in low spirits, are like hot water to a frozen limb.
Benjamin Rush

Mirth is God's medicine. Everybody ought to bathe in it. Grim care, moroseness, anxiety—all this rust of life—ought to be scoured off by the oil of mirth.
Henry Ward Beecher

We have a lot of evidence that shows mirth and laughter affect most of the major physical systems of the body.
Dr. William F. Fry, Jr.

Frame your mind to mirth and merriment,
Which bars a thousand harms and lengthens life.
William Shakespeare

Mirthfulness is in the mind and you cannot get it out. It is just as good in its place as conscience or veneration.
Henry Ward Beecher

Mirth can be a major tool for insight, changing "ha-ha" to "aha."
Joel Goodman

Meat eaten without either mirth or music is ill of digestion.
Sir Walter Scott

Prepare for mirth, for mirth becomes a feast.
William Shakespeare

nonsense

non•sense *n* words or actions that convey an absurd meaning or no meaning at all

---

Nonsense is used to point to the beyond of rational sense.
Christmas Humphreys

Nonsense is so good only because common sense is so limited.
George Santayana

Forgive me my nonsense as I also forgive the nonsense of those who think they talk sense.
Robert Frost

Don't talk to me about a man's being able to talk sense; everyone can talk sense—can he talk nonsense?
William Pitt the Elder

To appreciate nonsense requires a serious interest in life.
Gelett Burgess

A little nonsense now and then is relished by the wisest men.
Roald Dahl

It is far, far better to have a firm anchor in nonsense than to put out on the troubled seas of thought.
John Kenneth Galbraith

Nonsense is an assertion of man's spiritual freedom in spite of all the oppressions of circumstance.
Aldous Huxley

play • playful • pleasure • pun

play *vi*   *1.* to move rapidly or lightly, flutter   *2.* to amuse oneself, as by engaging in sport or a game; take part in recreation   **play** *n*

play•ful *adj*   fond of fun or play; frisky

Life should be lived as play.
Plato

I still get wildly enthusiastic about little things. . . . I play with leaves. I skip down the street and run against the wind.
Leo Buscaglia

A playful attitude is best.
Dr. Harold Bloomfield

The true object of all human life is play. Earth is a task garden; heaven is a playground.
G. K. Chesterton

Play and pray; but on the whole do not pray when you are playing and do not play when you are praying.
Charles Williams

Life is the sacred mystery singing to itself, dancing to its drum, telling tales, improvising, playing.
Manitonquat

To play is to yield oneself to a kind of magic.
Hugo Rahner

Play: Work that you enjoy doing for nothing.
Evan Esar

Play skillfully with a loud noise!
Psalms 33:3

We live in an ironic society where even our play is turned into work. But the highest level of existence is not work: the highest level of existence is play.
Conrad Hyers

The play concept . . . is of a higher order than . . . seriousness. For seriousness seeks to exclude play, whereas play can very well include seriousness.
Johan Huizinga

Man only plays when in the full meaning of the word he is a man, and he is only completely a man when he plays.
Friedrich von Schiller

You can discover more about a person in an hour of play than in a year of conversation.
Plato

If animals play, this is because play is useful in the struggle for survival; because play practices and so perfects the skills needed in adult life.
Susanna Miller

Unlike children in other countries, the Eskimos played no game of war. They played with imaginary rifles and harpoons, but these were never directed against people but against the formidable beasts that haunted the vast wastes of their land.
Marie Herbert

It is paradoxical that many educators and parents still differentiate between a time for learning and a time for play without seeing the vital connection between them.
Leo Buscaglia

Play reaches the habits most needed for intellectual growth.
Bruno Bettelheim

The ability to play is essential to being a creative artist.
Dewitt Jones

Necessity may be the mother of invention, but play is certainly the father.
Roger von Oech

If I had a party to attend and didn't want to be there, I would play the part of someone who was having a lovely time.
Shirley MacLaine

We do not stop playing because we grow old; we grow old because we stop playing.
Anonymous

When you're depressed, the whole body is depressed, and it translates to the cellular level. The first objective is to get your energy up, and you can do it through play. It's one of the most powerful ways of breaking up hopelessness and bringing energy into the situation.
Dr. O. Carl Simonton

You are led through your lifetime by the inner learning creature, the playful spiritual being that is your real self.
Richard Bach

The human need to play is a powerful one. When we ignore it we feel there is something missing in our lives.
Leo Buscaglia

The world is your playground. Why aren't you playing?
Ellie Katz

pleas•ure *n*   a feeling of enjoyment; satisfaction; delight

---

Most of us miss out on life's big prizes. The Pulitzer. The Nobel. Oscars. Tonys. Emmys. But we're all eligible for life's small pleasures. A pat on the back. A kiss behind the ear. A four-pound bass. A full moon. An empty parking space. A crackling fire. A great meal. A glorious sunset. Hot soup. Cold beer. Don't fret about copping life's grand awards. Enjoy its tiny delights. There are plenty for all of us.
United Technologies Corporation

Man is the richest whose pleasures are the cheapest.
Henry David Thoreau

Pleasure is very seldom found where it is sought. Our brightest blazes are commonly kindled by unexpected sparks.
Samuel Johnson

God Almighty first planted a garden; and, indeed, it is the purest of human pleasures.
Francis Bacon

One of the greatest pleasures of life is conversation.
Sydney Smith

The great source of pleasure is variety.
Samuel Johnson

Visits always give pleasure—if not the arrival, the departure.
Portuguese proverb

A great pleasure in life is doing what people say you cannot do.
Walter Bagehot

Pleasure is the only thing to live for. Nothing ages like happiness.
Oscar Wilde

Pleasure is the object, the duty, and the goal of all rational creatures.
Voltaire

Surely a king who loves pleasure is less dangerous than one who loves glory.
Nancy Mitford

The rule of my life is to make business a pleasure, and pleasure my business.
Aaron Burr

Old age has its pleasures, which, though different, are not less than the pleasures of youth.
W. Somerset Maugham

We tire of those pleasures we take, but never of those we give.
J. Petit-Senn

The greatest pleasure I know is to do a good action by stealth, and to have it found out by accident.
Charles Lamb

The truth is I do indulge myself a little the more in pleasure, knowing that this is the proper age of my life to do it: and, out of my observation that most men that do thrive in the world do forget to take pleasure during the time that they are getting their estate, but reserve that till they have got one, and then it is too late for them to enjoy it.
Samuel Pepys

One of the many pleasures of old age is giving things up.
Malcolm Muggeridge

The spirit is often most free when the body is satiated with pleasure; indeed, sometimes the stars shine more brightly seen from the gutter than from the hilltop.
W. Somerset Maugham

Pleasure without joy is as hollow as passion without tenderness.
Alan Jay Lerner

Pleasures are like poppies spread—
You seize the flow'r, its bloom is shed.
Robert Burns

We may lay in a stock of pleasures, as we would lay in a stock of wine; but if we defer tasting them too long, we shall find that both are soured by age.
Charles Caleb Colton

pun *n*   a play on words; humorous use of a word or words which sound alike but have different meanings; a play on two or more possible applications

---

It was so quiet, you could hear a pun drop.
Arthur "Bugs" Baer

A pun is a short quip followed by a long groan.
Anonymous

A pun is the lowest form of humor—when you don't think of it first.
Oscar Levant

A pun is a pistol let off at the ear; not a feather to tickle the intellect.
Charles Lamb

Good poets have a weakness for bad puns.
W. H. Auden

Hanging is too good for a man who makes puns; he should be drawn and quoted.
Fred Allen

silly • smile

sil•ly *adj* showing little sense, judgment, or sobriety; foolish, irrational, stupid, absurd, ludicrous

---

Nothing is more silly than silly laughter.
Catullus

We find it hard to believe that other people's thoughts are as silly as our own, but they probably are.
James Harvey Robinson

The "silly" question is the first intimation of some totally new development.
Alfred North Whitehead

Mix a little foolishness with your serious plans: it's lovely to be silly at the right moment.
Horace

smile *vi*   to have a facial expression in which the corners of the mouth curve upward and the eyes sparkle, that usually shows pleasure, affection, amusement, friendliness or, at times, irony or derision   **smile** *n*

Sex is the most fun you can have without smiling.
Madonna

A smile costs nothing but gives much. It enriches those who receive without making poorer those who give. It takes but a moment, but the memory of it sometimes lasts forever. None is so rich or mighty that he can get along without it and none is so poor that he cannot be made rich by it. A smile creates happiness in the home, fosters good will in business and is the countersign of friendship. It brings rest to the weary, cheer to the discouraged, sunshine to the sad and is nature's best antidote for trouble. Yet it cannot be bought, begged, borrowed, or stolen, for it is something that is of no value to anyone until it is given away. Some people are too tired to give you a smile. Give them one of yours, as none needs a smile so much as he who has no more to give.
Anonymous

She gave me a smile I could feel in my hip pocket.
Raymond Chandler

Smiling as if she had teeth of sugar that were always melting.
Rainer Maria Rilke

A smile appeared upon her face as if she'd taken it directly from her handbag and pinned it there.
Loma Chandler

A laugh is a smile that bursts.
Mary H. Waldrip

Laughter is regional: a smile extends over the whole face.
Malcolm de Chazal

The world always looks brighter from behind a smile.
Anonymous

Start every day with a smile and get it over with.
W. C. Fields

If you don't start out the day with a smile, it's not too late to start practicing for tomorrow.
Anonymous

No matter how grouchy you're feeling,
You'll find the smile more or less healing.
It grows in a wreath
All around the front teeth—
Thus preserving the face from congealing.
Anthony Euwer

If I can make people smile, then I have served my purpose for God.
Red Skelton

A smile is the universal welcome.
Max Eastman

A smile is an inexpensive way to improve your looks.
Charles Gordy

Wrinkles should merely indicate where the smiles have been.
Mark Twain

A smile confuses an approaching frown.
Anonymous

Keep smiling—it makes people wonder what you've been up to.
Anonymous

You're never fully dressed without a smile.
Martin Charnin

It takes seventeen muscles to smile and forty-three muscles to frown.
Anonymous

All the statistics in the world can't measure the warmth of a smile.
Chris Hart

If you would like to spoil the day for a grouch, give him a smile.
Anonymous

If you can smile when all else is going wrong, you must be a plumber working for triple time on a Sunday.
Anonymous

A smile is a light on your face to let someone know you are at home.
Anonymous

The bitterest misfortune can be covered up with a smile.
Yiddish proverb

What I saw was equal ecstasy:
One universal smile it seemed of all things.
Dante

There are no language barriers when you are smiling.
Allen Klein

'Tis easy enough to be pleasant,
When life flows along like a song;
But the man worth while is the one who will smile
When everything goes dead wrong.
Ella Wheeler Wilcox

It is impossible to persuade a man who does not disagree,
but smiles.
Muriel Spark

The hardest thing you can do is smile when you are ill, in pain, or depressed. But this no-cost remedy is a necessary first half-step if you are to start on the road to recovery.
Allen Klein

Better by far you should forget and smile
Than that you should remember and be sad.
Christina Rossetti

The fruit of love is service. The fruit of service is peace. And
peace begins with a smile.
Mother Teresa

Let a smile be your umbrella, and you'll get a lot of rain in your
face.
Gary Rabinowitz

The subtlest play of the zygomaticus major—one of the facial
muscles that govern the smile—can spell the difference between
the passing indifference of strangers and the flowering of lifelong
romance, the difference between peaceful coexistence and
deadly violence.
Dr. Melvin Konner

A smile is a curve that sets everything straight.
Phyllis Diller

A smile is a powerful weapon; you can even break ice with it.
Anonymous

Often truth spoken with a smile will penetrate the mind and
reach the heart; the lesson strikes home without wounding
because of the wit in the saying.
Horace

A smile is a passport that will take you anywhere you want
to go.
Anonymous

Smiles reach the hard-to-reach places.
Steve Wilson

When people are smiling they are most receptive to almost
anything you want to teach them.
Allen Funt

Let me smile with the wise, and feed with the rich.
Samuel Johnson

wit • witty

wit *n*   the ability to make lively, clever remarks in a sharp, amusing way

wit•ty *adj*   having, showing, or characterized by wit; cleverly amusing

---

Brevity is the soul of wit.
William Shakespeare

Being witty is like push-ups or jogging. If you work at it hard enough you improve.
Page Smith

Chaplin and Keaton developed wit and ingenuity the way other men develop muscles.
Molly Haskell

Wit has truth in it; wisecracking is simply calisthenics with words.
Dorothy Parker

Wit, by itself, is of little account. It becomes of moment only when grounded on wisdom.
Mark Twain

Wit consists of knowing the resemblance of things which differ and the difference of things which are alike.
Madame de Staël

Wit is the sudden marriage of ideas which before their marriage were not perceived to have any relationship.
Mark Twain

Wit is so shining a quality that everybody admires it; most people aim at it, all people fear it, and few love it unless in themselves.
Lord Chesterfield

Wit ought to be a glorious treat, like caviar. Never spread it about like marmalade.
Noel Coward

Wit is the salt of conversation, not the food.
William Hazlitt

When the wine is in, the wit is out.
Thomas Becon

True wit is Nature to advantage dress'd,
What oft was thought, but ne'er so well express'd.
Alexander Pope

You can pretend to be serious; you can't pretend to be witty.
Sacha Guitry

Wit is a sword; it is meant to make people feel the point as well
as see it.
G. K. Chesterton

Use your wit as a shield, not as a dagger.
American proverb

Wit's an unruly engine, wildly striking
Sometimes a friend, sometimes the engineer.
George Herbert

All wit rests on a cheerful awareness of life's incongruities.
George Will

The real wit tells jokes to make others feel superior, while the half-wit tells them to make others feel small.
Elmer Wheeler

Witty people may be neurotic, but they're not as likely to be psychotic.
Dr. Martin Grotjahn

Many live by their wits but few by their wit.
Laurence J. Peter

The greatest advantage I know of being thought a wit by the world is that it gives me the greater freedom of playing the fool.
Alexander Pope

Of course, it's very easy to be witty tomorrow, after you get a chance to do some research and rehearse your ad libs.
Joey Adams

Instead of working for the survival of the fittest, we should be working for the survival of the wittiest; then we can all die laughing.
Lily Tomlin

Wit is the only wall
Between us and the dark.
Mark Van Doren

In the end, everything is a gag.
Charlie Chaplin

INDEX TO AUTHORS

Caesar, Sid, 13, 14
Callahan, John, 18, 136
Camus, Albert, 66
Carlin, George, 15
Carlyle, Thomas, 113
Carson, Johnny, 58
Catallus, 168
Cerf, Bennett, 122
Chamfort, Sébastien, 126
Chandler, Loma, 171
Chandler, Marilyn R., 81
Chandler, Raymond, 171
Chaplin, Charlie, 10, 21, 185
Charnin, Martin, 173
Chekhov, Anton, 66
Cherbuliez, Victor, 53
Chesterfield, Lord, 181
Chesterton, G. K., 102, 154, 182
Chinese proverb, 59, 60, 114, 116
Churchill, Winston, 29
Cicero, 104
Clark, Frank A., 97
Clay, Andrew Dice, 14
Cleese, John, 88, 130, 131
Clemens, Samuel, *see* Mark Twain
Colby, Frank Moore, 87
Coleridge, Samuel Taylor, 57
Colette, 93
Colton, Charles Caleb, 163
Connolly, Cyril, 58
Coren, Alan, 107
Corinthians, 34
Cosby, Bill, 134
Course in Miracles, A, 62

Cousins, Norman, 86, 127
Coward, Noel, 46, 181
Cox, Harvey, 19, 138, 139
Crawford, Michael, 109
Crist, Judith, 58

Dahl, Roald, 151
Dalai Lama, 69
Dana, Bill, 128
Dane, Frank, 32
Dangerfield, Rodney, 15
Dante, 175
de Bono, Edward, 95
de Chazal, Malcolm, 171
Declaration of Independence, 52
de Mondeville, Henri, 117
Dentinger, Ron, 95
Dewar, Thomas Robert, 108
Dickson, Paul, 41, 45
Diderot, Denis, 21
Diller, Phyllis, 17, 127, 176
Disraeli, Benjamin, 3
Dr. Seuss, 44
Dostoyevski, Fyodor, 132
Dryden, Phyllis Campbell, 133
Durante, Jimmy, 131
Durrell, Lawrence, 107
Durst, Will, 137

Eastman, Max, 92, 101, 124, 172
Eberhart, E. T. "Cy," 91
Ecclesiastes (Old Testament), 120, 144

Ecclesiasticus (Apocrypha), 117
Eden, Emily, 32
Eisenhower, Dwight D., 96
Eliot, T. S., 126
Ellwood, Robert, 110
Emerson, Ralph Waldo, 2, 142
Emery, Stewart, 38
Emmanuel, 111
English prayer, 46
English proverb, 115, 141
English rhyme, 145
Ephron, Nora, 53
Epictetus, 71
Erhard, Werner, 72
Esar, Evan, 77, 155
Euwer, Anthony, 172

Fadiman, Clifton, 103
Feather, William, 26
Feigelson, Sheila, 93
Feldman, Marty, 14
Fielding, Henry, 37, 50
Fields, W. C., 171
Fitchner, Edward, 10
Ford, Henry, 65
Frank, Anne, 59
Franklin, Benjamin, 29, 32, 52, 113
Freeman, Kathleen, 14
Freud, Sigmund, 31, 93
Frost, Robert, 64, 106, 150
Fry, Christopher, 15
Fry, William F., Jr., 91, 95, 127, 146

ABOUT THE AUTHOR

Allen Klein calls himself a "jollytologist." He publishes an annual mail-order catalog that's appropriately named *The Whole Mirth Catalog* and has written a book, *The Healing Power of Humor*, that provides practical advice and humorous how-to's. Klein, a nationally recognized speaker, lectures and presents workshops on healing humor, how to bring more laughter into your life, and other laughing matters. For more information about his programs, contact him at 1034 Page Street, San Francisco, California 94117.